The Town Mouse and the Country Mouse

with

The Eagle and the Man

Illustrated by Val Biro

Award Publications Limited

A poor country mouse lived in a ditch. It was very ordinary, but he had made it his home.

    One day he wrote to his friend the rich town mouse and invited him to dinner.

    He thought his friend would enjoy the peace and quiet of the countryside.

The town mouse came,
but he did not like the country.

"You should visit me. Town is much more exciting than here."

So the country mouse went to stay with the town mouse.

The country mouse had never seen so many houses.

The town mouse's house was the largest of all!

The town mouse led the way to the kitchen. There was so much food, the country mouse could not believe his eyes.

The mice sat down to dinner.
The country mouse was very hungry after their journey.

Just then, a man came into the room to sweep the floor.

"Mice!" boomed the man's voice. The two friends ran into the mouse hole to hide.

When it was quiet, the mice left their hiding place. By now they were very, very hungry. Luckily the food was still there.

But the man had only gone away to fetch a dog to catch the mice. The frightened mice ran to hide again.

The mice went to bed hungry.

"I'm going home."

The next morning, the country mouse said goodbye to his friend.

He did not like the town at all.
So he ran all the way back to his home in the country.

"I may be a poor, simple country mouse, but at least I can live and eat in peace," he thought, as he dozed happily in the afternoon sun.

The Eagle and the Man

A great eagle was once caught in a net. He tried to get free, but the net was too strong.

A young man saw the eagle and went to help. He cut through the net and set the eagle free. He had saved its life.

Later that day, the eagle saw the young man asleep in the shade of a crumbling stone wall. The eagle could see that the old wall might fall down.

He wanted to repay the man's kindness. He swooped down and took the man's hat.

The young man woke up and chased after the eagle. He saw that it was the same eagle he had saved earlier that day.

"Come back!" he shouted.

In time, the eagle dropped the hat. The man wondered why the eagle had taken it.

He went back to the wall to finish his sleep.

When he saw that the wall had fallen down, he knew the eagle had saved his life.

The eagle had returned the young man's good deed.